Hope Packs for a Trip

A Book about Sorting

BY CHARLY HALEY

Published by The Child's World®
1980 Lookout Drive • Mankato, MN 56003-1705
800-599-READ • www.childsworld.com

Photographs ©: PR Image Factory/Shutterstock Images,
cover (foreground), 3, 5, 9, 13, 17, 18; Africa Studio/
Shutterstock Images, cover (background), 1, 6 (left), 10
(background), 14; Shutterstock Images, 2, 6 (right), 7,
11, 15, 23; Jeffrey B. Banke/Shutterstock Images, 10
(foreground); India Picture/Shutterstock Images, 20

ISBN HARDCOVER: 9781503824881
ISBN PAPERBACK: 9781622434237
LCCN 2017964156

Printed in the United States of America
PA02387

About the Author

Charly Haley is a writer and children's book editor who lives in Minnesota. Aside from reading and writing, she enjoys music, yoga, and spending time with friends and family.

Today was
a big day
for Hope.
What
did Hope
do today?

Hope packed things to prepare for a trip.

Hope's suitcase

Mom's suitcase

Hope and her mom had to **sort** their things into two suitcases.

One suitcase was for Hope.

The other was for her mom.

Mom's suitcase

The **laptop** computer belongs to Hope's mom. Hope put the laptop in her mom's suitcase.

The toys belong to Hope.
Hope put the toys in her
own suitcase.

Hope's
outfits

The trip will last for three days. Hope looked in her closet. She grabbed three **outfits**.

Hope put her outfits in her own suitcase. Hope's mom's clothes went in the other suitcase.

Now Hope is ready to go on a trip with her mom.

When do you sort things?

Words to Know

laptop (LAP-top) A laptop is a computer that is small and light. A laptop is easy to carry around.

outfits (OUT-fits) Outfits are sets of clothes to be worn together. Outfits might include shirts, pants, socks, and shoes.

sort (SORT) To sort is to put things into different groups. People sort their clothes after washing them.

Extended Learning Activities

1. Have you ever had to sort your clothes or toys? How did you sort them?

2. Why do people sort things? How can sorting be helpful?

3. Why would Hope and her mom sort their things into different suitcases?

To Learn More

Books

Jocelyn, Marthe. *Sam Sorts*.
Plattsburgh, NY: Tundra Books, 2017.

Peppas, Lynn. *Sorting*. New York, NY:
Crabtree Publishing, 2010.

Rice, Dona Herweck. *Sort It!* Huntington Beach, CA:
Teacher Created Materials, 2015.

Web Sites

Visit our Web site for links about sorting:

childsworld.com/links

Note to Parents, Teachers, and Librarians: We routinely verify our Web links to make sure they are safe and active sites. So encourage your readers to check them out!